Globalization
and
Childhoods

GLOBALIZATION and CHILDHOODS

"Let's play Princesses... I will be Princess Elsa and you can be Anna..." Mei Ling offered generously to her classmate. This was the aftermath of the Walt Disney animated movie "Frozen". Every little girl wanted to be Princess Elsa. No matter what apparent ethnicity she already was, she was ready to be the blond blue-eyed princess that was the heroine in the animated film. These girls were from a preschool in Singapore, having some time for their make-belief and pretend play.

"I want to be a lawyer when I grow up...", proclaimed one of the boys in the group while another quipped ambitiously "I will be the next prime minister..." after their teacher had a lesson activity with the group of 5 year olds about the roles of people in different occupations.

These anecdotes tell us of how children are in the process of forming the perceptions of their own identities, with influences coming from their environment, their peers, the media and the adults in their lives. Early childhood is therefore a critical period for the nurturing self-identity, self-esteem and confidence in positioning themselves as social beings in society. Just as children themselves construct their own identities, adults too respond to children and implement pedagogy based on their constructs of childhood (Sorin & Galloway, 2005). The social and cultural construction of children and childhoods are grounded based on the varying perceptions in different societies, cultural practices, values, epochs of history in a diversity of circumstances, experiences and contexts in which childhood is experienced (James & James, 2012; Jenks, 2004). The many varied social constructions of childhood include: the innocent/evil child, the noble child, the miniature adult, the agentic child, the child as a victim, the child as a commodity, the out-of-control child, amongst several others (Branscombe et.al., Levy & Orlans, 2004; 2000; Sorin & Galloway, 2005; Woodrow, 1999).

This theoretical paper will look at the many images and identities of childhood both from the adult and the child's perspectives. It will discuss childhoods as a social and cultural construction and also how children define themselves. Due to global inequalities, the expectations and reality of childhood in different cultures range on a spectrum with the inequality gap between the rich and the poor at risk of being exacerbated because of the effects of globalisation (Jones, 2005; Thompson, 2012). Thus, childhood in a poverty stricken third world developing country will vastly differ from that of the privileged modernized nation. The growing interconnectedness globally between different cultures involving linguistic, cultural, political and social ideologies (Robinson & Diaz, 2005) have resulted in increased diversity within the classroom and children who have experienced and lived in multiple cultural and geographical settings. The gap between the parents' and the child's sense of cultural identity is often an issue as host cultures often dominate the heritage and original cultures of the parents.

Who is the Child?

The United Nationals Conventions Rights of the Child (1989) defines the child as anyone from birth to the age of 18 unless the laws in a particular country defines the legal age for adulthood as earlier. However, the voting age, the age at which a driver's licence can be issued, the age of consent and the age when compulsory school can discontinue varies in different countries. The term 'child' carries certain specific legal implications; for example, the age of criminal responsibility varies from country to country. In countries where marriage is permissible at a younger age than 18, such as 12 for girls and 14 for boys in South Africa and Chile, the onset of adulthood is regarded as earlier with marriage implying the onset of adulthood (Morrow, 2011). These transition ages have been largely determined by the adults in the society and not by the children themselves.

As Loris Malaguzzi presented at Reggio Emilia (1993), there are multiple images of the child that directs the adult to relate to the child accordingly, as to the internal conception of what the child is. Based on this conception of what is child learner is and is capable of, the adult nurtures a learning environment that corresponds to this image. The quality of interactions and relationship with the child or children will also be reflective of the conceived image of the child learner.

Historical Influences

Historically, over the centuries, there are a few beliefs and conceptions about the young child in

Western society that have shaped traditional discourses about the development of the child. Thomas Hobbes (1588-1699) believed that development was about socialising children to take their roles within society and that the young child is wild and unregulated in the original natural state. John Locke (1632-1704) who was an academic, doctor, philosopher and political theories constructed the idea of the child as a 'tabula rasa' or with a mind that is a blank slate ready to receive knowledge through the senses which is converted to understanding through the application of reason. In the book, Emile, Jean Jacques Rousseau (1712-1778) created the image of the innocent child whose development is fostered through protection and nurturing whilst allowing free, undirected exploration and play. Other philosophers and educators that have been influential throughout the centuries include Emmanuel Kant (1724-1804), Johann Pestalozzi (1746-1827), Friedrich Froebel (1783-1852), John Dewey (1859-1952) amongst several others (Feeney et. al., 2010). The philosophies and these cultural-historical influences continue to influence and impact early childhood educators' work with young children, their families and the communities that they live in.

Social, Cultural and Narrative Constructs

Based on Vygotsky's social constructivist theory, the child's development and self-identity is influenced and shaped by their social and cultural environment, of which interactions and relationships with others such as parents, carers, siblings and peers scaffold their learning and acquisition of skills (Stemmel, 2002; Woodhead, 2006). Therefore, as social and cultural practices are different in various cultural communities, development is impacted by these differences (Rogoff, 2003). For example, children's learning in different communities can be in the form of formal schooling, working and helping out on a farm or apprenticeship and development in these communities is through the natural social and cultural participation in community activities.

Childhood can therefore be viewed as social phenomena as communication and relationships are social processes and enacted through group play, patterns of social behaviour and consumerist popular culture of toys, entertainment and media in modern environments (Kehily and Swann, 2003). Early childhood has been perceived and interpreted differently in different societies and various epochs of history, geographical locations and differentiated based on gender, ethnicity, income status which also mark the inequalities that are found in childhoods locally and globally (Montgomery et.al., 2003). From international and global perspectives, there has been renewed debate on how children should be viewed and regarded. Up till more recently, Eurocentric perspectives have been the predominant approach to how childhood is constructed and when or how developmental milestones should be reached.

As elaborated a little later, personal and social identities in childhood are co-constructed through their interactions with others in shared activities, role and pretend play, communication and non-verbal interactions and possibly later through social media and the experience of everyday conflicts are the origins of self-identity in childhood (Dunn, 2004). It is through day to day narratives when children weave their personal stories into personal narratives that play a role in the constructing, deconstructing and reconstructing their own unique narrative identities through a variety of voice, both their own and through others (Bakhtin, 1981; Kristeva, 2000). Children's identity formation occurs through the telling and retelling of everyday personal experiences and events, and creating stories during their play and social interactions, reading and listening to stories in children's literature.

The Impact of Globalization

The child, childhood and child development has more recently been viewed and interpreted through the lens of globalization (OECD, 2012; Ruddick, 2003). Although globalization has caused a prevalent image and vision of what childhood is, the universalization of approaches to the child contradicts what we understand about contextualisation, the unpredictability of human nature and the effects of the availability resources (Task, 2010). The current dominant conceptualisation and image of the child regarding the representation and the nature of childhood is largely a Western hegemonic one which is being transmitted across different cultures. Whilst cultural and historical constructs of the child has been the subject of debate and contention with scholars, the corporate world has also used the construction of childhood to create and sustain a consumer idea and ethic through the media, movies and new technologies (Kincheloe,

2002). Children are also in the position of having the power to create their own discourse and corporations like Disney have presented 'ideologically loaded' and a 'global subconscious colonization' to consumers, both children and their families (Fleer et. al., 2008; Kincheloe, 2002). Both the positive and negative influences of globalization continue to impact the everyday lives of families and young children through political, economic and cultural changes and transformation, their learning tools, increased residential relocations and migration, together with the progressive awareness of their rights as persons and individuals.

Global Inequalities

In the everyday lives of children, there is a wide spectrum of difference in different geographical locations around the world. Inequalities in terms of resources, environments and cultural expectations are often widened. The access to technology, computers and the internet have caused children and youth in modern societies to become influenced by contemporary consumerist cultures and also equipped them with a new interactive form of communication and learning through personal mobile devices and apps (Thompson, 2012).

In contrast to these affluent, advanced, Westernized images of the privileged child is that of the images of third world child poverty (Ruddick, 2003). As observed by Punch and Sugden (2013), the roles of children and youth in communities in Vietnam, India and China are changing. Traditionally, children make a critical contribution to providing sibling care, collecting water, cooking and cleaning. With rural locations, children are involved in work such as tending to fields, other agricultural tasks and other forms of responsibilities that contribute to the livelihoods in their communities. In the past decade or so, there has been changing patterns and gradual transformation in almost all communities with progressive urbanisation and modernisation (Punch & Sugden, 2013). This has been accompanied by an increasing emphasis placed on education and schooling for the children in these societies

Identity Development

Identity is a legal concept that is defined by the UN Convention on the Rights of the Child and is every child's entitlement from birth (United Nations,

1989, Article 7.1). The UNICEF Innocenti Research Centre (2002) documented that in 2000, approximately 50 million babies which is more than two fifths of births were unregistered. Legal identity as a right is established from birth whilst personal, social and cultural identity develops throughout a person's life. Gender, ethnicity and religion are some of the factors that influence and shape how a child views himself or herself in relation to others (Morrow & Connolly, 2006). The family, society and community, together with associated conflicts and inequalities that the child may experience through discrimination or exclusion will mould and influence the child's developing identity and their sense of belonging (Rogoff, 2003).

Cross-cultural and third culture children and youth face number of challenges when it comes to self-identity as they have lived and spent much of their developmental years in multiple cultures (Nguyen & Benet-Martinez,2010). It would be difficult to assign a 'pure identity' to these children and it is more often a complex identity is developed that is composed of hybrid or multicultural identities because of the internalisation and influences of two or more cultures (Schuff et. al., 2016).

A child's identity may be differentiated into personal and social identities and these identities are developed through the roles, activities and relationships with peers, parents, teachers and others in the child's everyday environment at home, preschool and the community (Dunn, 2004; Woodhead, 2008). It has more recently been acknowledged that the Western ethnocentric concept of a stable and individualised universal model of the process of development of self-identity is not entirely accurate and identities in modern culturally diverse societies are dynamic and multifaceted that develop through changing cultural and social contexts and the variety of human experiences (Brooker & Woodhead, 2008). Identities are therefore negotiated through the language or languages, the cultural values, practices and beliefs in the child's environment. It is also nurtured and co-constructed through the narratives and interactions between themselves, their peers and the adults in their lives.

Needs vs Competencies

If the image of the needy and vulnerable child is associated with protection rights, then the image of the competent and 'rich' child is consistent with participatory rights. It is true that children of minority of low socio-economic status, disability require the mediation and protection of adults or authoritative organisations which emphasizes their dependencies and vulnerabilities. The other view of the child as "…image of the child is rich in potential, strong, powerful and competent…" (Malaguzzi, 1993) supports the UNCRC Articles 12,13,14,15 that advocates the freedom of expression, thought, conscience and having their own views and privacy in accordance to the child's evolving maturity and intellectual capacity. Following Vygotsky's socio-cultural theory, there is the view that children's competencies can be developed through guided participation in the community of learners so that their skills and competencies can be 'scaffolded' and guided by a more skilled or competent adult or peer.

Cross-cultures and Third Cultures

It is also because of globalisation and with its effects of increased international mobility that has allowed people and their families to cross geographic borders and relocate. The children who have accompanied their parents and families and lived most of their childhood and young lives in a country or countries that are foreign to both their parents' cultures are know as third culture kids or TCKs for short. The term 'third culture' was first coined by sociologists, Useem and Hill (1993) who were interested in the phenomena of people with high mobility, who regularly crossed borders and whose occupational roles involved relating to two or more cultures. These children with their families live in a highly mobile way of life and have to adjust to changes in location, cultural norms and practices, values, language and education structures and systems (Pollock and Van Reken, 2009).

In terms of research themes on TCKs, the most distinguishing one are that on the language adjustment issues and that of identity positioning of these children. The issue of cultural identity has been most perplexing because the TCK's cultural identity has been described as that which is a complex and dynamic interplay of language, blended and/or shifting cultural identities and belonging, together with emotional issues interwoven together (More and Barker, 2012; Tannenbaum & Tseng, 2015).

Cross-cultural children as opposed to third culture kids are children of immigrant families who have moved to a new culture with a more permanent settlement in mind. Traditionally, it has been easy to differentiate between these two groups because TCKs are children whose location is due to the career choices of their parents while cross-cultural children are immigrants who have moved permanently to a new culture. This definition issue was brought up by Pollock and Van Reken (2009). A person or a child's culture is a critical element of their identity formation, contributing to their self-identity and also influences their social or group identity. Sometimes, these individuals have experienced and lived in multiple cultures and places during their developmental years so much so that they develop the ability to 'shift identities' depending on the cultural setting that they are in.

Cultural Diversity and Language Identities

It has been said that language is intrinsically connected to culture, performing the social function of communication of societal group values, norms, beliefs and nurtures the sense of group belonging and identity (Bakhtin, 1981; Baker, 2001). Preserving and protecting the language and therefore identity rights of children of minority or indigenous groups has not always been a successful endeavour. A child's right is to their identity and language, and to experience and preserve their own cultures even if parents and families are under the pressures of assimilation and acculturation into the dominant national cultural and language identity. Language although not the sole continent factor in self-identity has been acknowledged as an integral aspect of national identity. Children have been known to possess multiple linguistic identities as in the case of many third culture children. Bilingualism and even multilingualism has been viewed as the alternative in many modern nation-states.

In order not to frame research based on an Eurocentric ethnocentric perspective, many researchers have positioned themselves based on global-local viewpoints, including childhood and childcare practices in rural communities. This generates a diversity of cultures and perspectives of research so that a wider and greater understanding of children and childhood is gained. The vast gap between the childhoods of the privileged capitalist societies and that of the Third World developing country is a reminder that the definition of childhood and the child cannot be universalised. However, it is with some irony that economically, child poverty is becoming more and more a common occurrence in the US and European countries where the existence of children is an progressively reliable predictor of household poverty (Ruddick, 2003). For educators and the curriculum, understanding the connectedness between identity, culture and language is particularly important for those who work with culturally diverse learners.

TCK & the Multilingual English Language Learner

'Hannah'

Hannah is 6 years old this year. She has been with the preschool center since she was a toddler (around 2 years of age) and has been going there five days a week, usually between eight in the morning to about half past four in the evening. Her father is Scandinavian whilst her mother is Japanese. The family has been living in Singapore for the past 7 years since her parents relocated when her father landed the contract with his current multinational company. She is the elder of two children and her younger brother is still less than 18 months old. Both parents are working professionals although her mother works mainly from home. Hannah's mother travels back to Japan a few times a year. Hannah accompanies her mother or parents occasionally on such trips to visit her grandparents. She speaks English at home, particularly with her father but will converse with her mother in Japanese. She has recently also begun Japanese language classes at a private language center. According to Hannah, both her parents will individually spend time with her reading before bedtime about once a week. Hannah enjoys dressing up and trying various types of fashion. She likes helping her mother prepare meals at home. On her literacy habits, Hannah enjoys both informative books and those of imaginative stories, particularly those based on some popular animated movie titles. She enjoys reading and browsing through books on her own but likes it particularly when her parents read with her. Her father reads to her in English whilst her mother tends to explain and converse with her in Japanese.

Hannah walks to school with her mother with her younger brother in a stroller. They arrive at about quarter past eight every morning. As her mother speaks to the infant care staff, Hannah walks in confidently with her bag. She goes to her classroom and puts her things in her cubby hole before joining the other children in the communal dining area. "You know, I will be going with my mother to Japan next week," she smiles happily at the thought of it. "What are you going to be doing there?" asked her classmate. "Oh, I will be visiting my grandparents". Later that afternoon, the teacher gets the class to do a choral reading response to the story Brown Bear Brown Bear, what do you see? Hannah remarks, "That's an easy book, I can read that." After the reading, the teacher gets the class to write their own story using the phrase 'What do you see?' Hannah goes about the task without asking too many questions. Roy asks "How do you spell Scorpion?' then Harry asks "How do you spell yellow?'. "*Aiyah… Y – E – L – L –O-W same as the yellow in yellow duck," responds Hannah. The children continue write their lines into their books. "I'm done!" says Hannah and passes her book to the teacher for checking. "That's fast but a little too brief… where is your question mark and line spacing, Hannah?" asks the teacher.

Commentary: Hannah is not your typical child attending preschool in Singapore although the enrolment in the center has mostly children from the local community. She was enrolled in the same center since she was two-year-old. Hannah has been relative fast in adapting and learning both English and Chinese while immersed in the bilingual curriculum which is found in most local Singapore preschools although neither her parents' first language is English or Mandarin. Her proficiency in the English language is above average compared to her peers within the same age group in the center despite mostly speaking to her mother in Japanese at home. This is probably attributed to the fact that she spends five full days in the preschool center where equal amounts of time are spent learning or interacting in both languages of the curriculum with her class teachers and peers and her parents spend time reading with her. She has also just started going for Japanese language classes once a week. She looks forward to attending an international school in the following year.

The issue of language acquisition by Hannah may have been quite different should she have come into the preschool at a slightly later stage or maybe even at primary/elementary school level. This is because the two-year old child is at a stage where he or she is just beginning to develop and practice oral language skills, so Hannah integrated into the bilingual curriculum quite easily at this early stage. The center has the policy of not teaching the children any Chinese pinyin or phonetics till the year before they enter primary school and when the children are usually more confident in their level of mastery of English phonemic awareness.

Hannah was able to learn through the cross-cultural experience through the centre's programme that also integrate cultural diversity of the difference local ethnic races through various activities such as interactive cultural theme boards, celebrating racial harmony, international friendship days and many of the major local festivals in Singapore such Chinese New Year, Deepavali, Hari Raya and Christmas. She gets along well with her preschool classmates and her sense of belonging came from developing friendships with the peers in her class who were mainly from the local community. She also enjoyed playing 'big sister' to many of the younger children in the center. Of course, her sense of identity may be disrupted when she transits from preschool to her new international school environment where she would then be immersed in a more international culture. Her ability to communicate in English, Mandarin and Japanese will probably put her in a good position to develop cross-cultural friendships through her communication skills. Her next challenge would probably be to adjust to her new school environment and to develop new friendships with those in her new school as she transits to Grade 1 or elementary school.

TCK or Third Culture Kids was a term that was first coined by the sociologist Ruth Hill Useem in the 1950s. The home culture of the parents is referred to as the first culture, the host culture to which the family has moved to, as the second culture while the third culture refers to the interstitial culture that usually are shared commonalities of expatriates who were living an internationally mobile lifestyle. This third culture is neither similar to those of the parents' home culture nor that of the local community (Pollock et. al., 2017). When both parents are from different cultures who have moved to another community abroad that is different from either their homes cultures, then things become even more complex as the diverse cultural experiences make these definitions even more complicated

Part of the definition of a TCK or third culture kid is that of "…someone who has spent most of his or her developmental years outside their parents' culture" The third culture child is vulnerable as they undergo a cross-cultural experience during the developmental years of their lives when their sense of cultural identity and relationships with others is particularly important during their formative years. Culture and language is something that is learnt and assimilated from one's environment and the people around them (Hiebert, 2008). In the TCK, through their parents, caregivers, peers, school, their home, 'passport' culture, the media and the third or interstitial culture.

Language Acquisition

The practical advantage of the TCK is that they usually acquire fluency in more than one language because of their cross-cultural upbringing. Children, in particular, learn two or more languages quickly when they are exposed to the languages regularly in their home and school settings. Thus, bilingualism or even multilingualism is not an uncommon trait in TCKs and is seen as an advantage in not only communicating with different cultural groups or persons, and in some cases, appears to give them an edge in academic learning. However, in the initial stages, before the TCK is able to acquire sufficient proficiency in the school language, they may be assessed as 'delayed' in the linguistic domain based on traditional assessment. This despite the fact that the bilingual or trilingual child may have a greater vocabulary and overall linguistic ability than their monolingual peers. The main challenge or issue in acquiring multiple languages at an early age is that sometimes, the TCK does not always become proficient enough to be critical thinkers in more than one language. Bilingual language acquisition during childhood can be simultaneous or sequential, also known as consecutive and successive (Baker, 2006). Vygotsky's social cultural theory points to the crucial role of social-cultural interaction in the development of cognition and language in a child and this occurs through everyday interactions and activities with parents, caregivers, teachers, peers and other in the child's environment.

Language and Identity

Third culture children are well-known to be able to shift and blend identities in a multicultural setting and usually develop a strong sense of intercultural competence (Moore & Barker, 2011). On the flip side, the third culture child can also be vulnerable to an identity crisis. It has been documented that when the families are repatriated or return back to their parent's home country to live , they may find that the dominant society will validate only one aspect of their cultural identity and they may be unable to integrate within the dominant culture (Fail, Thompson &

Walker, 2004). For example, it has been noted that in the past, Japanese who return to their home country known as 'kikokushijo' were not viewed in a positive light as conformity in Japan is seen as a positive trait (Brislin, 2000; Fail et. al., 2004).

The language or languages spoken by a person plays a significant role in determining the sense of cultural identity or identities. While English is viewed as a globalized or international language, just about 5.5% of the global populations have some degree of proficiency in its use (Robinson & Diaz, 2006). Language is viewed as a critical marker of identity and identity is indistinguishably connected to the ways through which we understand ourselves and others.

REFERENCES:

Baker, C. (2001). *Foundations of Bilingual Education and Bilingualism.* (3rd ed.). Cleveland: Multilingual Matters.

Baker, C. (2006). *Foundations of bilingual education and bilingualism.* Toronto: Multilingualism Matters Ltd.

Bakhtin, M. (1981). Discourse in the Novel. In *M.M. Bakhtin: The Dialogic imagination. Four Essays*. Austin: University of Texas Press.

Branscombe, N. A., Dorsey, A. G., Surbeck, E., & Taylor, J. B. (2000). *Early Childhood Education - A Constructivist Approach.* Boston: Houghton Mifflin Company.

Brislin, R. (2000). *Understanding culture's influence on behaviour.* (2nd ed.). Fort Worth: Texas: Harcourt.

Dunn, J. (2004). *Children's Friendships: The beginning of Intimacy.* Malden, MA: Blackwell.

Fail, H., Thompson, J., & Walker, G. (2004). Belonging, identity and third culture kids:life histories of former international school students. *3, 3*, 319–338.

Feeney, S., Moravick, E., Nolte, S., & Christensen, D. (2010). *Who Am I in the Lives of Children.* New Jersey, Columbus, Ohio: Merrill.

Fleer, M., Heregaard, M., & Tudge, J. (2008). Constructing Childhood: Global-Local Policies and Practice. In *Childhood Studies and the Impact of Globalization:*

Policies and Practices at Global and Local Levels (pp. 1–20). Taylor & Francis.

Hiebert, P. (2008). *Transforming worldviews: An anthropological understanding of how people change.* Michigan: Barker Academic: a division of Barker Academic Group.

Hill Useem, R. (1993). Third culture kids: Focus of major study. *Newspaper of the International School Services, 12*(3).

Hill, L., Stremmel, A. J., & Fu, V. R. (2005). The Child as a Cultural Invention. In *Teaching as Inquiry; rethinking curriculum in early childhood education* (pp. 77–92). Pearson/Allyn & Bacon.

James, A., & James, A. (2012). *Key Concepts in Childhood Studies* (2nd ed.). UK London: SAGE Publications Ltd.

Jenks, C. (2009). Constructing Childhood Sociologically. In *An Introduction to Childhood Studies.* (2nd ed.). Maidenhead.: Open University Press.

Jones, G. A. (2005). Children and Development: Rights, Globalization and Poverty. *Progress in Development Studies, 5*(4), 336–342.

Kincheloe, J. L. (2002). The complex politics of McDonald's and the new childhood: Colonizing Kidzworld. In *Kidsworld childhood studies, global perspectives and education.* (pp. 75–122). New York: Peter Lang Publishing.

Kristeva, J. (2000). *Hannah Arendt: Life is a narrative.* Toronto, ON: University of Toronto Press.

Levy, T., & Orlans, M. (2004). Attachment Disorder: Antisocial Personality and Violence. *Annals of American Psychotherapy Association, 7*(4), 18–24.

Mercuri, S. P. (2012). Understanding the Interconnectedness between Language Choices, Cultural Identity Construction and School Practices in the Life of a Latina Educator. *GIST Education and Learning Research Journal, 6,* 12–43.

Montgomery, H., Burr, R., & Woodhead, M. (Eds.). (2003). *Changing Childhoods: Local and Global.*

Moore, A. M., & Barker, G. G. (2011). Confused or multicultural: Third culture individuals' cultural identity. *International Journal of Intercultural Relations, Article in Press.*

Moore, A., & Barker, G. (2012). Confused or multicultural: Third culture individuals' cultural identity. *International Journal of Intercultural Relations, 36*(4), 553–562.

Morrow, V., & Connolly, P. (2006). Editorial. *Children and Society, 20,* 87–91.

Nguyen, A. M. D., & Benet-Martinez, V. (n.d.). Multicultural identity: What it is and why it matters. *The Psychology of Social and Cultural Diversity.,* 87–114.

Pollock, D. C., & Van Reken, R. E. (2009). *Third culture kids: The experience of growing up among worlds.* (Third). Boston, MA: Nicholas Brealey Pub.

Pollock, D. C., Van Reken, R. E., & Pollock, M. V. (2017). *Third Culture Kids: Growing Up Among Worlds.* (Third). Boston: USA: Nicholas Brealey Publishing.

Punch, S., & Sugden, F. (2013). Work, education and out-migration among children and youth in upland Asia: changing patterns of labour and ecological knowledge in an era of globalization. *The International Journal of Justice and Sustainability.*, *18*(3), 255–270.

Robinson, K. H., & Diaz, C. J. (2006). *Diversity and difference in early childhood education: Issues for theory and practice.* Berkshire, England: Open University Press.

Robinson, K., & Diaz, C. J. (2005). *Diversity and Difference in Early Childhood Education: Issues for Theory and Practice.* McGraw-Hill Education.

Rogoff, B. (2003). *The Cultural Nature of Human Development.* Madison New York: Oxford University Press.

Ruddick, S. (2003). The Politics of Aging: Globalization and the Restructuring of Youth and Childhood. In *Antipode* (pp. 334–362). Oxford UK; Malden USA: Blackwell Publishing.

Sanders, B. (2009). Childhood in Different Cultures. In *An Introduction to Early Childhood Studies* (2nd ed., pp. 53–64). SAGE Publications.

Schuff, H., Hogskole, A., & Sykekehusi, S. (2016). Supporting identity development in cross-cultural children and young people: resources, vulnerability, creativity. *Scandinavian Journal of Intercultural Theory and Practice*, 3(1).

Sorin, R. (2005). Changing Images of Childhood: Reconceptualizing Early Childhood Practice. *International Journal of Transitions in Childhood*, 1.

Sorin, R., & Galloway, G. (2005). Constructions of Childhood: Constructions of Self. Presented at the Childhoods 2005 International Conference, Oslo, Norway.

Stremmel, A. (2002). Nurturing professional and personal growth through inquiry. *Young Children*, 57(2), 62–70.

Swann, J. (2003). *Childrens Cultural Worlds*. (M. J. Kehily, Ed.). John Wiley & Sons.

Tannenbaum, M., & Tseng, J. (2015). Which one is Ithaca? Multilingualism and sense of identity among third culture kids. *International Journal of Multilingualism*, 12(3), 276–297.

Thompson, R. A. (2012). Changing Societies, Changing Childhood: Studying the Impact of Globalization on Child Development. *Child Development Perspectives*, 6(2), 187–192.

UNICEF Innocenti Research Centre. (2002). *Birth registration: Right from the start* (Innocenti Digest No. 9). Florence.

Woodhead, M. (2005). Early Childhood Development: A Question of Rights. *International Journal of Early Childhood, 37*(3), 79–98.

Woodhead, M. (2006). *Changing Perspectives on early childhood: theory, research and policy.* (Background paper for the EFA Global Monitoring Report 2007 No. 33). UNESCO.

Woodhead, M. (2008). *Developing Positive Identities.* (L. Brooker, Ed.). The Open University.

Woodrow, C. (1999). Revisiting images of the child in early childhood education: Reflections and considerations. *Australian Journal of Early Childhood, 24*(4), 7–12.

www.ingramcontent.com/pod-product-compliance
Lightning Source LLC
Chambersburg PA
CBHW051404250726

48656CB00006B/2261